Remembering Lee

Remembering Lee:

The noblest
revenge is
To forgive.
—Thomas Fuller

Paige S. McLemore

XULON PRESS

Endorsements

In her book "Remembering Lee: A Sister's Journey of Obedience and Faith", Paige McLemore shares her story of growing up in a normal, average American home. Surrounded by a loving family, she experienced the ordinary ups and downs of life until the unimaginable happened. With great transparency, McLemore reveals the lowest moments of her life and the hopelessness that kept her bound for years. Her downward spiral would have ended tragically without Divine intervention. The transforming power of God found in her Savior Jesus Christ radically changed everything. Anger, bitterness and hopelessness was changed to peace, forgiveness and hope. This inspirational, transformational story is for everyone who has lost hope but still hasn't given up.

Office of the Executive Director
W. Thomas Hammond, Jr.
Georgia Baptist Mission Board
6405 Sugarloaf Parkway
Duluth, Georgia 30097
770-936-5203

One of the hardest things we will ever do in life is to offer forgiveness to someone who doesn't want it. Though unique and heart-wrenching, Paige's story is your story, and it's mine. Life eventually leads each of us to that crossroad of forgiveness or bitterness. This book serves as a guide to our own personal journeys in a way that is raw and honest as we face the inevitable decision of carrying the weight of unresolved hurt or offering grace where it is undeserved.

Jeff Bumgardner
Worship Pastor | FBC North Augusta, SC

Paige's story of obedience and faith after the murder of her sister is too powerful not to share. However, it is hard to write a book like this because it exposes you to the world. There is no place to hide the details of the "messy middle" between the hurt of the loss and the healing of God's love. The first time Paige shared the story of her sister's murder with me, I immediately felt the power of both the loss and the journey after the loss.

As a father of two girls, I see the benefits my girls experience each day from their relationship as sisters. I can't imagine one of them going through life without the other. Paige and her sister had that same type of unique bond. **Paige will tell you that she was the jokester and that her sister was the thinker. However, you will quickly realize that Paige is as thoughtful as anyone you have ever met. Her conversational, fun- loving, southern personality will jump**

off the page. You will feel her struggle with the question "why" and the movement toward a settled feeling of peace. As Paige wrestles with God's leading to forgive the man who murdered her sister, God provides clarity and direction.

This book contains a story about the significant power of loss and pain that connects with any reader. Pain is the common ground on which all humanity stands. As you begin your journey through this book, consider these words from Dr. Norman Geisler. "*Life is not skipping from mountain top to mountain top. There are valleys.*" For many of us, the valleys are where we meet the people who hurt us most deeply. Paige leverages the power of her painful journey to remind the reader that "*the noblest revenge is to forgive.*"

Dr. Stephen Cutchins
Senior Pastor | FBC North Augusta, SC

Xulon Press
2301 Lucien Way #415
Maitland, FL 32751
407.339.4217
www.xulonpress.com

Unless otherwise indicated, Unless otherwise indicated, all Scripture quotations are taken from the Holy Bible, New Living Translation, copyright © 1996, 2004, 2007, 20134 by Tyndale House Foundation. Used by permission of Tyndale House Publishers, Inc., Carol Stream, Illinois 60188. All rights reserved.

Printed in the United States of America.

Paperback ISBN-13: 978-1-6628-0379-6
Ebook ISBN-13: 978-1-6628-0380-2

DEDICATION:

I want to dedicate this book to my husband, Steve, and our son, Blake. Thank you for allowing me the time to write. Thank you for always being in my corner and for loving me just as I am.

To Steve, thank you for reminding me to "never ring the bell" and to face my fears head-on. Without your love and encouragement, I would not have written this story to inspire others to forgive. You are my love.

To my mom and dad. I hope this book reminds you that there is life after tragedy and sorrow. Our lives were forever changed, but the hope that comes from Jesus Christ will sustain us until we are all called Home. We will see Lee again. I can hear the angels singing now. What a reunion that will be for you both. I love you with all my heart.

To my praying circle of friends: Rhonda, Tina, Wanda, Caroline, and Kim. Thank you for your prayers, your group texts, your encouragement, your "let's meet in the library" prayer time, and for your laughter and love. Your friendship is a reminder of God's faithfulness and love for His Kingdom's daughters. Without all of you, I would be lost.

And finally, thank you, Pastor Stephen. You have spoken prophecy over me in so many ways. Thank you for believing in me and investing your time to tell my story. You were the first to push me to teach God's word and to pursue my dreams of sharing my story. Thank you for your counsel and for your friendship.

Thank you Lynn for always "holdin on to me!" I love you!

CONTENTS

FAITH

1

1

~

FAMILY

**Searching and shame say I am guilty,
but grace says I am free.**

As I sit down to write this book, I bow my head and pray, *God, write this book for me; no fear, just faith.* This prayer speaks to my life in so many ways. For as long as I can remember, fear of every kind has been a factor in my life: fear of being alone, fear of not measuring up, fear of not being popular enough or pretty enough, and especially fear of not being worthy of God's love. If you have ever felt this way, I pray that my story will help you *fearlessly* accept God's love, His indescribable grace, and help you pursue the life He has promised you. I pray that you will seek His plans for your life today. Don't wait, as I did. Seek Him now.

Have you ever pictured yourself in a church business meeting? Me either. But that is just where I was on a random Tuesday a few years ago. One day during a discipleship meeting, I was asked to attend a business meeting at church for an upcoming event. First of all, the fact that

I was going to a church business meeting is hysterical. God does have a sense of humor, doesn't He? Our interim pastor, Stephen, led us through a passage in Matthew chapter 5 before the official meeting began. This passage speaks of revenge and how it is not up to us to seek it. As I sat there and listened to him, the Holy Spirit rose in me like never before. Before I knew it, I blurted out that I knew this passage because I had lived it. I rambled on about how I'd had a sister who was murdered. I spoke about how my life had changed because of Jesus and how much I loved Him. The pastor and everyone else in the room had no idea about my sister. The looks on their faces were priceless.

Stephen looked at me and said, "Well, we need to get that on video! This is too powerful not to share with the world." Those words were the beginning of my new adventure, my new life in Christ. God was only beginning to show me how exciting and unexpected it can be to follow Him. The Holy Spirit needed me to blurt out in that business meeting. He needed me to obey His prompting. He needed to show me that He will never break a promise. God promises us that if we are in the business of glorifying Him with our experiences, our actions, our words, He is in the business of making our lives abundantly more than we can ever imagine. And that was exactly what was happening to me that afternoon in that meeting and is still happening to me today.

I grew up in Augusta, Georgia, the youngest of four girls. Our three-bedroom, one-and-a-half bath brick home was full. My parents worked hard to give us what we wanted. We always had what we needed. I barely remember my two older sisters, Debra and Angel, living with us. They were older when my parents married and had moved out by the time Lee and I were in grade school. Our house was loud and full of laughter just as you expect from a home full of girls. My poor daddy had to put up with all the drama that all of us girls demand. I had a great childhood.

After Debra and Angel moved out, I vividly remember Lee and I getting our own rooms and thinking we were so grown up. You see, Lee and I were only fourteen months apart in age, and were often mistaken for twins. We were inseparable. It is funny how we both felt so grown up with our own rooms, but I always ended up sneaking in Lee's room to sleep. In the evenings, we would lie in Lee's bed and watch our little black-and-white television. Y'all remember the little radio televisions with the antenna; that is such a 1980s memory. I try to explain to my son what it was like to have to actually get up and change the television channel. He will never understand the greatness of the 80's. Lee and I would watch one of the only three cable channels available and talk late into the night.

When it was time for lights out, we would say our prayers together. Lee would begin, "Now I lay me," then I would chime in, "down to sleep." Lee's turn, "I pray the Lord my soul to keep." Back to me, "if I should die before I wake, I pray the Lord my soul to take." Randomly, we would take turns "God blessing" the ones we loved and always ended in unison with, "and don't let the bed bugs bite!"

I distinctly remember after our prayers were finished one particular night, Lee said something I can't forget. She said, "I am scared to go to sleep some nights because I am afraid I will forget to breathe." I assured her that was silly and that she would wake up; to not worry about such things.

I wondered, *Why did she say that?* Why in the world would a pre-teen girl say such a thing? Looking back, I wonder now why I didn't question her about it. You see, Lee was a thinker and she was always cautious about things. I remember my parents having to calm her each morning before taking us to school. My parents asked a pharmacist friend to make a fake concoction of "medicine" for Lee. We called it, "I have to go to school medicine." It was nothing but sugar water with green dye, but Lee would take it in the mornings before school and it calmed her fears. You have to admit, that was a pretty smart idea.

Ironically, there have been times since Lee's death when I have had the same thoughts about forgetting to breathe; especially when I remember her. The pain of losing her is so deep and embedded in the corners of my soul that I have to remind myself to take a breath, to wake up from the nightmare of horrific memories. The manic questioning of: *Why is she gone? Why did she have to leave me? Why am I alone? Why did God do this? What did I do to deserve this?*

I now think that it is not a silly fear at all, to think that you will forget to breathe. In fact, it is a reality of my life since the day Lee was taken from me.

Elizabeth Lee Shields was smart, kind, and reserved. She was the girl everyone wanted to befriend. Lee was level-headed and sensible. She obeyed curfew, made good grades, and lived her life as an example to her friends. Growing up, our mom would frequently tell the story of carrying Lee on her hip as the doctor told her she was pregnant again. That would be me. I was the surprise child; Lee was going to be a big sister. My unexpected birth brought a child who was the complete opposite of her mild-mannered big sister. Loud, gregarious, and always the center of attention, that was the personality God gave me. Although we were very different, Lee and I perfectly complemented one another. We shared secrets, friends, and dreams; we were a team.

Our little middle-class family was not perfect, but it was full of love, laughter, friends, and happiness. Our parents made sure we had dinner as a family every night and were in church on Sunday mornings. We did our homework at the dining room table, said blessings at dinner, and our prayers at night.

As Lee and I grew into teenagers, sharing clothes and a bathroom brought its typical battles, but Lee and I remained close. With our differing personalities, I began to feel the need to protect Lee, to take up for her when she needed it. I do not know why I felt that way; she was perfectly capable of taking care of herself. I was loud, and she was reserved. I aimed to be the center of attention, and she aimed to be valedictorian of her class. I was a jokester, and she was a thinker.

As I look back, I realize that although I had a larger personality, I actually felt inferior to Lee. In fact, if I am being completely honest, I felt inferior to many of our friends. I always felt like I was not smart enough, or pretty enough, or popular enough. Never in a million years would I have admitted this then, but I did. I used my gregarious personality to cover up my insecurities. If I was hurt, I laughed and made a joke out of it. How many of us do this? I am sure many can relate. If I was mad, I let you know it, not caring whose feelings suffered because of it. This flaw in my personality became more apparent after Lee was gone and drove my self-destructive behaviors and insecurity for years.

I guess in my eyes, Lee was the better sibling. She made better grades, had more success, and better hair. I saw how everybody loved her, wanted her to be around her, and admired her. I admired her too. I counteracted that with mediocre grades, seeking attention in all the wrong ways, and bad perms. Lee made good, sound choices; I made stupid mistakes. I can recall one night when my best friend, Lynn and I went to a party. Lee was there too of course. Being careless, I damaged my parents' car. I drove it home. I am sure I was also late. I crawled into bed with Lee and begged her to take the blame. Certainly, Mom and Dad would not punish her as much as they would me. I was sure I had long ago run out of chances with them. Thankfully, Lee agreed.

However, the next morning, Lee went out to see what she was going to confess to and quickly recanted her offer, saying, "no way, I'm taking the blame for that one!" Yep, it was pretty bad, and yep, I was grounded.

I tell you this story because I think it speaks to how I felt about myself, how at times I still feel about myself. I automatically thought our parents wouldn't be angry with Lee because she was the better person, daughter, and child. My parents gave me no reason to believe this, it was just something inside of me.

I wondered, *Why did Lee agree to take the blame in the first place? Did she realize I had used up all my chances? Did she realize how I felt about myself?* She probably just felt sorry for me. I guess I will never know. What I do know is that Lee and I were as close as two sisters could be, and we loved each other very much! As I think back to that time, it makes me smile. We had the house where all our friends came to hang out. My mom had all the snacks, the love, and the patience for us and all our friends. We had a great little life in that little brick home.

Jeremiah 17:7
But blessed are those who trust in the Lord
and made the Lord their hope and confidence.

Those insecurities still show up. They show up at work, at church, in social settings. However, now that I know Christ and His Word, I see them in a different light. I know that Satan gets in my head and wants me to feel like I don't measure up. He wants me to feel like I am not worthy. Has he ever done this to you? God's Word tells us that Satan is the father of lies. He whispered lies to me for years, but God has given me the truth. He has written the truth on my heart . . . permanently. My confidence should always come from Christ. Our confidence should always come from Christ alone.

As a young girl, I wished I had had someone to pour God's word into me. Maybe it would have changed things after

Lee's death. That is one reason I am writing this book today. I want you to know that we are loved. We are beautifully and wonderfully made. The Lord is enthralled with our beauty. As much as we try, we cannot do things on our own. We must always remember that although we think we can do it on our own, we are only strong when we are in Christ. We are enough for whatever life throws at us when we are in Christ. He makes us whole, beautiful, and resilient. Our confidence must be in Jesus Christ . . . every day and at every moment. And besides, I never met a strong person with an easy past. Read that one again.

My dear friend, Wanda, gave me a book of Psalms and she marked one especially for me. It is priceless to me. This Psalm is for you as well. Soak it up and never forget it. Write in on your heart. You are beautiful. We belong to our Lord and Savior, Jesus Christ.

Psalm 45:11, 13–14
The King is enthralled by your beauty, for
He is your Lord ... All the glorious is the princess
within her chamber; her gown is interwoven with gold.
In embroidered garments, she is led to the King.

2

~

ABSENCE

God's silence does not mean His absence.

THURSDAY

After high school, both Lee and I enrolled at Augusta College, the local university. Lee was progressing through her sophomore year and I was a freshman. We both worked part-time after classes at locally run businesses. We were well on our way to adulthood. We shared classes and dreams. Lee aspired to have a career as a dental hygienist; I, on the other hand, had no idea what I wanted to do with my life. Each day, we rode to class together, discussing typical sister topics: boys, fashion, Fred Couples, and the future. Yes, I said Fred Couples; yes, the golfer. Lee loved him. She followed his career and even met him. He was very special to her. What a story she had to tell!

After classes, she would drop me off at the local Hallmark cards store at a nearby shopping center where I worked, then she would go to the local sporting goods store where she worked. The sporting goods store was owned by our neighbor and close friend.

Fall was in the air. It was Thursday, October 26, 1988, a cool day in Augusta. I only recall the weather because I remember what Lee wore that day. She had on a new pair of jeans, a beige cropped sweater, and new brown boots. She was perfectly dressed in all that 1988 fashion had to offer. We went to class, home for lunch, and we were off to work. It was a typical day for us.

As I began my normal working routine, I found it strange when the girl I was friendly with, from the dress shop next door, came over and frantically asked how to work my cash register. A moment later, the shop phone rang. The voice on the other end was my dad.

"Paige, Lee has been shot, your Granny will pick you up. Meet us at the hospital!"

Click! My head was spinning. As I looked at the girl from the neighboring shop, I knew it was serious by the look on her face. She looked horrified. She frantically yelled, "Just go, we heard there was a robbery at the store where Lee worked on the radio!"

I often think of her and how terrified she must have been. She knew I was working alone that day and would need someone there to relieve me. I am thankful for her quick thinking, and more importantly, her actions. As I ran out of the card shop, I saw my grandmother pulling up. I jumped in the car and we sped off to the hospital. I do not think we said a word to each other the whole way there. We walked into the hospital and were immediately shuffled back to this small room where my parents sat in shock. Together, we waited in that cold, bare room.

Lee had been immediately taken to surgery. The horrible truth was that Lee had been shot in the head. And even knowing this truth, I still held out hope that she was going to be just fine. We stayed in that room for hours. At one point, I opened the door, only to see hundreds of our friends sitting in the corridor of the hospital. There were so many people sitting on the floor, crying, worried, the image remains in my mind's eye. Lee was loved; it showed in the hearts of our friends that day.

We eventually were moved to another waiting area where we could have a few visitors at a time. My two best friends, my grandparents, and close family friends were allowed to come and sit with us. That day was long, confusing, and chaotic. I recall my mother just sitting, crying, and sobbing. We went home late that night to change and try to rest, hoping that Friday would bring a miracle.

It did not.

Death penalty may be sought in Johannsen's robbery case

By Cas Shearin
Staff Writer

District Attorney Sam B. Sibley Jr. said Monday that he "absolutely" will consider seeking the death penalty against 19-year-old MacArthur Lawton Jr., charged with armed robbery and murder in last week's double slaying at a Washington Road sporting goods store.

"Obviously in a case that is as brutal as this one, the death penalty would certainly be considered." Sibley said.

He said his office hasn't received a file on the case yet, but he anticipates reviewing the case later this week. "I hope to be in a position to tell you later in the week, after I've had a chance to look at the reports," he said.

The prosecutor said he will make a decision on whether to seek the death penalty before he presents the case to a grand jury.

"You've got to consider whether the case qualifies, because there are certain things that must be present before you can even

consider asking for the death penalty, and these things must be considered in laying out the form of the indictment," he said.

In Georgia, at least one aggravating circumstance must, be present before a jury can return a sentence of death. Aggravating circumstances include: murder during commission of armed robbery, kidnapping, rape or another murder; murder for the purpose of receiving money or anything of

See DEATH, Page 6A

Mom and Dad met with the doctors and were faced with a decision I would not wish on anyone. Lee was on life support and could not survive without it. The doctors asked my parents to decide if and when to take her off life support. I remember family members asking a million questions at the same time. *Can we just take care of her and leave her on life support? Maybe she will live? If we did leave her on life support, what kind of quality of life will she have? What would Lee want?* All I knew for sure was that I wanted to see Lee. I wanted to see her before any decisions were made. *Maybe she would wake up. Maybe she would live. Maybe she would recognize my voice.* My parents agreed to let me go back and see Lee with my older sister Angel.

I walked back to the intensive care room. Lee was lying still, bandaged, and hooked up to lots of equipment. My sister was unrecognizable. To this very day, the image remains at the forefront of my memory. It will never leave me. At that moment, the true horror of the situation became all too real.

The movies do not portray what really happens when someone is shot. They glorify people in hospital rooms talking to their injured loved ones, begging them to wake up. The movie victims are usually in full makeup with fake wounds and great hair. I don't watch those kinds of movies anymore. People say I am a wimp. If they only knew what I saw that day, they would not be so quick to judge me. What I live with, what I lost, what I saw with my eighteen-year-old eyes remains *indescribable*. Robin Williams once said, "Everyone you meet is fighting a battle you know nothing about. Be kind. Always." That is good advice for all of us. We go through our busy days thinking only of our needs and wants. A good friend once put it this way, " Everybody's got something." Try to remember that the person in line at the grocery store that pulled into your parking space, "they got something." Try to remember when your child's teacher forgets to return your email, "they got something." Always remember that those of us that know Jesus Christ as our Savior have something too. We have something so undeserved that we can freely give back, and that is God's grace. Give some grace today, afterall, we all got something.

As I write this, I see Lee as she was that day, and my heart is racing. These images will haunt me for the rest of my life; they will always rock me to the core. The pain lies on my chest and makes it difficult to breathe. The feeling is indescribable, just like the images in my mind. To this day, I have to directly speak to myself when these images flood back. I have to get them out of my head as soon as they pour in. There are nights when I beg God to relieve me of these memories. I have to strategically identify these thoughts and immediately ask God to remove them. He always does. Nevertheless, I will always be thankful for that moment with Lee. I told her I loved her and touched her face one last time.

Later that day, my parents made the most difficult decision a parent will have to make. They allowed doctors to remove Lee's life support.

Lee was gone.

I remember my dad coming out of the room. He did not have to say a word. We knew. He threw his hands up in the air and that was it. The room was filled with sobbing, so much heartache and raw grief. My reaction should not surprise you. I punched the wall, screamed, kicked, and cried. No one could control me. I remember my best friend Lynn trying to comfort me. At the time, I did not want anyone's help or comfort. I did not want anyone's help or comfort. The anger inside of me would not subside for years to come.

ALONE

Now what? What do you do after your sister is murdered? We went home. I went straight back to Lee's room and lay on her bed. But there was no time to mourn. I remember my parents scurrying around, calling the funeral director, and making plans for Lee's funeral. I remember people in our house. I recall Mom and Dad sitting me down and asking who I thought should be pallbearers for her funeral and what dress Lee should wear? What a decision for an eighteen-year-old to have to make. I had to pick out a dress for Lee to wear to her funeral. Just typing this gives me a lump in my throat. Things were going too fast. There was no time to grieve. There was no time to think.

Days later, the funeral was packed with family and friends. As we left the funeral home, my uncle Milton had to peel me off of the coffin where Lee was laid. I did not want to leave her. I did not want to be alone. I did not know how to live without her. Friends continued to flood us with food, cards, flowers, and visits. To this day, when I smell fresh roses, I am immediately carried back to the smell of my parents' home after the funeral. My husband knows that roses are off the flower list for me. The senses are a powerful thing; the scent of fresh roses is just too much of a reminder of this dark time in my life.

After a tragic death, family and friends show up, they do all they know how to do and then . . . it's quiet. Everyone goes back to his or her life, and you are left with silence. What do I do with this quiet? I remember after the funeral, the house was still full of people, overhearing my two older sisters saying that they were worried about me. They were concerned that Lee would always seem perfect to Mom and Dad and that would negatively affect me. They worried that I would feel like I would never be able to measure up to the memories of Lee. As I listened to their conversation, I thought *no way that would ever happen*. I loved Lee and would never feel like that. I think a lot of families face this problem when they lose a child. It isn't anyone's fault; it is just that everyone is in survival mode. Grieving parents are trying to cope with unimaginable loss; siblings are trying to cope with the pain of losing their companions and finding their identity in their "new normal." I struggled with wanting to talk about Lee but not wanting to upset my mom and dad. I struggled with the exact thing that my sisters were discussing. I did feel like I would never measure up but I could not verbalize it to anyone. So I just decided to be silent about Lee, silent about how I was feeling, just silent. It was a hard time.

As I look back, those concerned conversations would prove to be true in so many ways. For years, I would never admit that I felt that way; people would think I was a horrible person. They would think I was being a selfish person and a brat for even thinking that Lee was somehow responsible for me feeling inadequate. For years, I kept my mouth shut and tried to live my life without Lee and without anyone's help. The noise in my head would haunt me for years.

EMPTY CHAIR

After the funeral and the initial grieving period, we went back to school, back to work, back to life. Never mind not knowing how. *How do I live a life without Lee?* I was still numb and had no idea how to live. My first day back to school was life-altering. I drove to school in the car Lee and I shared. All those fights we had over who was driving did not seem to matter anymore. In fact, I was ashamed of those silly arguments. I parked and walked into the class Lee and I shared. I sat down in my seat, looked over at her empty chair, got up, and walked out. I felt the classroom's eyes on my back as I flung the doors open to that auditorium classroom. A cousin who also shared the same class followed me out. He tried talking to me, but I was unreachable. I was angry, alone, and hell-bent on not taking anyone's help or advice. No one had the right to tell me what to do. After all, they did not understand what I was going through.

That big auditorium classroom was filled with people, but I was alone. That empty chair in front of mine symbolized how alone I felt. Friends and family filled our home, but somehow, I felt alone. The person who had always been right beside me was no longer alive. I was alone with my thoughts, alone with my pain, along with my insecurities, along with my anger, alone with those terrible images of Lee in the hospital. The anger that caused me to punch that wall in the hospital the day Lee died was raging. I was alone, full of hate, and wanted revenge on the man who had killed my sister. I felt like a castaway. Too ashamed to admit it, I set out to prove my worth. If you have ever felt this way at some point in your life, keep reading.

Then came the murder trial. This moment in my life brought out the worst in me. We had to travel to Savannah because the courts felt the murderer would not get a fair trial in Augusta. The courtroom was filled with his family, my family, lawyers, and the jury; everyone looking through each other, no one recognizing the other person's pain. I sat in that cold, marble room for days and listened to the horrific details of Lee's murder. I listened to the testimony from a young woman who discovered Lee after she was shot. She sat on a stand and recited the gruesome details of how Lee looked, how she sounded. Those details still haunt me to this day. It was too much for a girl of eighteen years to handle.

My daddy had to sit on the stand, holding a photo of Lee and testify. I still don't understand why he had to testify. We were the victims; only it did not feel that way. The lawyer for the man who murdered Lee, his attitude, his words, they were judgmental and arrogant. His words and demeanor sent a wave of hate into my heart that would penetrate it for years. The only word that can describe my feelings in that courtroom is *hatred*. We hated them; they hated us. I looked at the man who murdered my sister and I hated him. He would not look at me. I wanted him to look at me so badly. It consumed me. After the verdict of life in prison, I ran out of the courtroom, enraged and emotionally scarred by the details I had been exposed to. I ran out screaming, kicking walls, and crying uncontrollably. A detective from Augusta took me into a room and attempted to calm me. I do not remember that detective's name now, but I have always wished to thank him for caring about me. He was very kind and genuinely concerned about me. His eyes seemed to feel my pain. I think he understood me more that day than anyone.

The following day, we packed up and went home. I do not remember ever discussing my breakdown with anyone, discussing the trial, or Lee, for years. My parents were in survival mode, and I was untouchable.

John 10:10
The thief does not come except to steal, and to kill, and to destroy. I (Jesus) have come that you may have life and that they may have it more abundantly.

The subtitles of this chapter I've called Absence are Alone and Empty Chair. They describe exactly how I felt. Maybe you feel this way now or have felt this way too. John 10:10 describes how Satan works. His only job is to kill, destroy, and lie to us. He is the thief who wants to take our happiness and joy. Satan stole Lee from us. He used that young man and his drug addiction and desperation to kill her. Satan wants us to feel alone, empty, and absent from the presence of God. He will do anything to keep us from God's promises. If you are feeling alone today, seek God's promises. If you are asking, how do I do that? Read God's Word. Immerse yourself in His Word and pray. He will be there. The second part of John 10:10 says that Jesus has come to give us abundant life. He wants to give me an abundant life despite what I was going through. I just needed to yield to Him. That is a wonderful promise from a loving God. I do not have to feel alone and empty ever again. And neither do you. Although I felt like God was a million miles away from me at this horrible time, I am certainly never absent from His presence. Jesus is and was always holding my hand. He will hold your hand too. Although I thought I was alone, He never left me. I would have given anything to have known this truth about Jesus back then. He would have saved me from all the heartache that came after Lee's death. But God never wastes a hurt, and He was not wasting this one for sure.

3

INSIGNIFICANT

God is not *A* source but *the* source of our souls' desires.

Insignificant is not a word I use often, especially about myself. However, as I reflect it seems fitting. Recalling the years I lost after Lee's death, I see that the mistakes I made are only attributable to my having minimal self-worth, no sense of belonging, feeling alone, and hurt. Struggling with being enough, even before Lee died, seemed to be in my DNA. In high school, I found that being loud and acting like the life of the party was where I found acceptance. People liked me, and that was what I wanted most. After Lee's death, it was the fuel Satan needed to defeat me, to rule over me. At the time, being enough meant that I had to be accepted in all social scenes. I believed I needed to be liked by others, no matter the cost. Now that Lee was gone, I added hate, anguish, anger, and bitterness to the low self-esteem cocktail. This combination created a world of heartache and self-destruction for me.

After Lee's death, I quit college. I found part-time jobs and lots of parties. Not believing that I had a great future or that anyone really cared, I was going through the motions of life. My feelings of insignificance and loneliness became my shield. I shoved all those feelings down and became someone that I don't even recognize today. I was loud, abrasive, and unashamed. As I look back, I should have asked for help, but that would have meant admitting I needed it. This was not an option for me. Who was going to listen? What was the point? Lee was not coming back. I was bound and determined to do things my way and without anyone's permission. Even at the expense of hurting myself and others along the way.

One of my biggest regrets was jumping into a marriage I was not emotionally prepared to handle. Besides the fact that we were both young, and I was a mess. The relationships the marriage brought into my life added to my insecurities. The feelings of not being good enough were fueled by the same social circles I so desperately wanted to be accepted into. I was in the center of a world where I did not belong; the more I tried to fit the part, the more I was excluded. People who were supposed to love me rejected me. Deep down all I wanted was to be loved, accepted, and have a family. However, I was alone and fighting to be accepted.

Have you ever thought you had to desperately fight to prove others wrong? I have. I felt like I had to prove my self-worth to others. The more others hurt me, the harder I fought. Sadly, oftentimes when striking back, I hurt myself and innocent bystanders. I was trying to force life and relationships, asking myself all along the way, *Why does this*

have to be so hard; where is the peace I so desperately want?
Well, it doesn't have to be so hard. We don't have to prove
our self-worth to others. The problem was that I did not
fit in. My path was supposed to be different. God never
intended for me to have to fight to be accepted. I wish I
understood that at the time. The good news is that I understand it now. Better late than never right? If you have ever
thought that you had to prove yourself to others, then you
need to hear this. Our identity is in Christ not in the things
or in the people of this world. Sure it is wonderful when
you surround yourself with trusting, loving, God-fearing
family, and friends. But the world doesn't always work that
way. We will tread in murking waters in this life. We have to
know where our true identity comes from, no matter what
situation we are in or who surrounds us. That is the beauty
of knowing Christ. We are not meant to fit in. As I have
grown, I now relish in being the outcast. I take extraordinary pride in the fact that God has not called me to fit in.
He has set me apart. In case you are wondering, He has set
you apart too.

You see, during this hard time, I knew right from wrong.
Deep down, I knew I was not living as God intended. I
knew the things I was accepting and doing were wrong.
What I did not know at the times was that Jesus has a beautiful way of cleansing your conscience. He gives us an aware-
ness of right and wrong. Jesus does this for us, not the world.
I was looking at the world to give me peace and a purpose,
and that's the wrong place to look every time. God gave
me the dream of having a family. However, I was so caught
up in trying to force that dream to become a reality that it
all blew up in my face. After lots of mistakes, the marriage

ended. Reflecting on this period of my life is hard because I know now that I hurt people who did not deserve to be hurt. I hurt myself. God hates divorce. It leaves a mark on your soul.

I wish I could say that I changed after the divorce, but I did not. I now added the shame of a divorce to all the other feelings of inadequacy bottled up inside of me. I recall meeting with my parent's church leader. I remember crying and asking her if God was mad at me. She assured me that God was not mad at me for getting a divorce. However, I did not believe her. I wish I did believe her, she was right. Unfortunately, things got worse.

Living outside of the will of God led to many disappointments and heartaches. The old song about searching for love in all the wrong places became my anthem. I spent the better part of the 90s and the first few years of the 2000s lost, alone, and hurt. I allowed men to treat me terribly. I allowed them to abuse me, both physically and emotionally. For me, emotional abuse is way harder than physical. The old saying, sticks, and stones will break my bones, but words will never hurt me, is a lie from Satan himself. Those dreams of having a family caused me to put up with being mistreated. I just knew that it was all up to me to find someone to marry and have a family no matter what I had to put up with to get it. I desperately wanted to be loved and to be a mom.

I just knew the time had run out for me. My life was going to be one disappointment after another. As I remember those hard years, I can see me as this lost little girl. I guess I am really remembering my heart. You know how you can feel your heart so strongly as if you can see it? I see my heart laid wide open with all the hurt exposed for the world to see. I trust no one. It stings to remember that season of my life. The shame and regret weigh heavy on my heart. I hate thinking about this time of my life. The beauty of Jesus is that the more I submit in Him, the less I dwell in the past. And that is what I want for all of you. I know someone reading this book will understand this next statement:

It is so hard when all your contemporaries are getting married, buying houses, and having babies and you are not.

My internal dialogue continued to speak louder than the truth. What did I do so wrong to not deserve a family who loved me, accepted me, and understood me? If this speaks to you, keep reading.

I felt like an outsider, a third wheel everywhere I went. I would be dateless at weddings, alone at showers, and bitter and envious at baby showers. Every occasion poured more salt into my deep, open wounds. I remember my best friend celebrating her twins' first birthday when I left the party in tears. I cried to her mother in the driveway. I was so bitter and desperate for a family. She tried to console me but I was inconsolable. Life was not fair was my only response to her kind words. I thought: *What did I do so wrong for God to not let me find happiness; why couldn't I be a mom; why does God love my friends more than me?* Events like these intensified my grief over what my life had become. I became more isolated.

I wanted a family. I wanted to be loved. I wanted to be a mother. I wanted to be settled. Don't we all? If you have ever felt unsettled, you'll know that it is a hard emotion. I could not stay at home because I did not want to be alone. But when I went out with friends, I still felt alone. Feeling unsettled is like a double-edged sword: one side leads to crying and sorrow and the other leads to regrets and mistakes. With nowhere to turn, I had no hope, or at least I thought there was no hope for me.

James 1:6
Be sure your faith is in God alone. Do not waiver.
For a person with divided loyalty is as unsettled
as waves being tossed by the wind.

What I have discovered was that I was being eaten up by this world that is ruled by Satan. He was trying his best to steer my internal dialogue towards hopelessness. He was doing a really good job too. The chief liar whispered these hopeless thoughts in my head for years. I would go out, wild as a buck, and come home only to cry myself to sleep. I would cry out into the night, *"I want my sister back! God, just give me my sister back!"* I thought I was all alone. I knew I wasn't living right, but I had no one to live right for. What was the point? I felt like nobody cared. I felt like everywhere I turned, no one understood. No one could say the right thing to me. People would say, "Everything happens for a reason," or "It is time to move on, Paige." These comments just made me angrier. I was that fly-off-the-handle girl, with no regrets. I was angry at the world, angry at myself, and angry at God.

The problem was that I *did* have regrets, I hated who I saw in the mirror, and I hated the man who killed Lee. I wanted peace, acceptance, and love, but had no idea how to find them or who to ask. I was trying to force relationships so that I could have that family I desperately wanted. I was lying to everyone, covering up my true feelings. I would try to talk about these feelings, but I could never express them correctly. What I know now is that God did not need my help. He just needed my obedience. He needed me to stop and look to Him for my significance, love, and acceptance. He needs that from you too.

I was searching for comfort in this world and that, my friends, is the wrong place to look. First John says that "we are children of God and that the world around us is under the control of the evil one" (1 John 5:19). I remember that I cried the first time I read this important verse. I never realized that Satan rules this world that we live in. It explains a lot about today's world, doesn't it? I wanted acceptance from people, but God needed me to seek acceptance from Him. He needed me to seek Him in the midst of this mess, not what the world had to offer. I now know that only God can provide what I desired. I need you to know this too. I do not doubt that I am *not* the only girl to ever go down this road. That is why I am writing this book. I need you to know that acceptance, the kind of acceptance that we yearn for, is only found in Jesus. He is not *A* source but He is *the* source of what our souls desire.

Oh, how I wish I knew that then. That empty, insignificant feeling consumed me, as it does so many. But knowing God's Word can change all of that!

You are not alone. Psalm 73 says, "Yet I still belong to You, You hold my right hand" (Ps. 73:23). Isn't that beautiful? It is the perfect picture of a Father holding His little girl's hands, 24/7.

I hope this word from our Lord gives you comfort. If we live each day with the desire to seek Him, He will fill up our hearts with abundant love for ourselves and others. Seeking the world's approval will only leave us disappointed and full of heartache. I had to learn this the hard way; I pray you do not.

2 Corinthians 1:3
God is our source of comfort.
Period.

TRUST

Jesus has the power to rewrite your HIStory.

After years of struggling and resisting the calling of the Holy Spirit, I could not ignore it anymore. Actually, He had pretty much been pounding on my heart, and I had to finally "call uncle" on my life as I knew it. Those regret-filled moments became more intense, as the Holy Spirit called me out of the darkness. Knowing God wanted more from me was undeniable. I think about all the times I ignored His calling, His yelling at me to stop and be still, and my refusal to hear Him saddens me. I am thankful for God's relentless love and patience with me.

Why did I ignore all the nudges, whispers, and flat-out yelling from the Holy Spirit for all those years? What makes us not want to change? How many people ignore the Holy Spirit's prompting their entire lives? God never gave up on me. He won't give up on you, either. God made every one of us, and He knows us better than we know ourselves. He stayed with me; He was persistent with me. God knows I am hard-headed however, I am not a match for the great I Am. His mercy and grace are nothing short of a miracle. Some say that God doesn't perform miracles anymore, but I say, you haven't met me.

To answer some of my rhetorical questions: we don't want to change because of our egos; we think our way is always the best, but it is not. Pride is the sin that keeps us all far from God. God says in Proverbs 16:18 that pride goes before destruction. Boy do I know that is the truth. Our prideful nature does not want us to change. Fear of the unknown, of change, drives our stubborn hearts. I was fearful of not having any friends, fearful of others not wanting to be around me if I chose Jesus. I lived with the fear of being rejected, of not fitting in.

I finally pushed myself to finish school and landed a job as an elementary school teacher. I loved my students and found purpose in my work. However, my personal life was a mess. I was lost. I was in and out of the church and searching. But what was I searching for? A wise co-worker that clearly knew the Lord, told me to be still. At the time, I did not understand what she meant. But those words would stick with me for years.

I wanted to love, to be loved, but I did not possess the power to make that a reality. One bad relationship followed another. It was a terrible cycle. I picked every wrong guy in the universe. I allowed them to treat me like dirt because of my desperate desire for a family. They took advantage of me and I allowed it. I became this needy girl who wanted so desperately to be accepted and loved. I wanted to drive a particular car, have a perfect house full of kids and dogs.

After every break-up (usually a horrific break-up), I would end up feeling like it was entirely my fault. I would spend countless days trying to win back these guys who had hurt me, apologizing to them for things *I did not do*.

I was broken and extremely tired of the fight. Thinking back on this time, honestly, embarrasses me. What was I thinking? I wonder why I am writing about it. The fear of being judged by my readers is real. I cannot let my fear dictate this book. I know that someone reading this book has been through similar experiences. **My desire to help others and to glorify God out weigh the fears.** The woman I am today would never beg for someone to love her. The woman God created would never allow herself to be mistreated. The power of the cross has cleared my eyes, and now I know my worth. Jesus taught me to be confident and sure-footed, not by my power but by His. Friends, if you have ever felt like this, there is hope, there is a future because *there is always Jesus.*

With this newfound confidence, I swore off dating. I was going to concentrate on my students at work. But God had other plans. A co-worker and her husband wanted to set me up on a blind date. Reluctantly, I agreed. I remember going to the University of Georgia football game to meet Steve and thinking this was a terrible idea.

My thoughts were: *He will never like me, I have a terrible past.*

Well, you know how God blesses you even when you are not so close to Him? That date changed my life. The moment I met Steve; I knew he was different. He had this assurance and calmness that immediately attracted me. He was confident and humble. The combination of these two traits is rare in today's world. He seemed interested in the real me. And guess what? He was nothing like the kind of man I thought I wanted all those years. Steve was different. I had hope.

After that football game, things began to change. Steve and I grew close. He said he loved me. I loved him. I really did. Despite these wonderful changes in my life, self-doubt and low self-esteem would rear their ugly heads at times. Satan was not going to give up on me. At night when I was alone, I would think: *How could he love me; I had a terrible past? How could he just love me; I have made so many stupid mistakes?* Our inner dialogue matters ya'll. It matters what we say to ourselves. That is why it is so important to know what God says about us. We can defeat Satan's whispers by responding with what God says.

There was no judgment from Steve; no questions about my past. He simply loved me. In fact, after dinner one night, I confessed to him some things about my past that I felt he needed to know. As I sat on my couch and cried to him, I remember his words clearly, "I am not interested in your past. We all have a past. I am not going anywhere. I love you."

For the first time in my life, I honestly believed it when he said he loved me. There was a calmness to our relationship that I had never experienced before—it was easy. God was showing me that it could be easy. I was so happy. The only problems that arose in our relationship came when I doubted Steve's love.

I remember one occasion when Steve sat me down and sternly said, "Paige, I love you. I am not from your past. Whatever has happened to you or been done to you, was not from me. You do not have to worry about me. I am not going anywhere." How many times do we bring trouble on ourselves because we keep bringing up the past?

God does not remember or sins, He tells us in Hebrews 8:12: "And I will forgive their wickedness, and I will never again remember their sins."

So why should we?

Steve is a quiet man, but when he speaks it is profound and direct. He means what he says and says what he needs to say.

Steve and I married one year after that first blind date. I had never been so sure of anything in my life. All those years of searching and struggling were finally over. We were happy. We were in church and making plans. And guess what, girls? We had a little country house on eight acres, with no central heating or air, a gravel driveway, a beat-up truck, a dog, and a cat. We were miles from a grocery store and nowhere near a country club or a cocktail party. Sometimes in life, the old dreams have to be taken away, so that the new dreams can come true. We were in my new little heaven. It was perfect.

God's dreams are better than our dreams. I've said it before and I will say it again: He knows us better than we know ourselves. God took me out of the rat race and placed me in a little eight-acre slice of heaven with a man who loved me as I deserved to be loved. Steve showed me that quiet nights in the woods, candle-lit dinners, and being still was much more fulfilling than nights out on the town. I grew to love getting my hands dirty and walking in the woods with our dog was way more fun than shopping at the mall.

Steve and I wasted no time preparing for a family. We were both in our mid-thirties and ready to be parents. We tried to get pregnant for months. I became discouraged when it didn't happen right away. Patience is not my thing and never will be. Steve of course, knew it would happen. I talked about it constantly with family and friends, searching for any advice. But God had other plans. He was teaching me to reach for Him.

The elementary school where I was teaching was being painted. When schools are painted, you get to know the familiar faces of the painters. It takes a long time to paint a school. Painters have to work around teachers, classes, and schedules. This particular year, a gentleman in the painting crew and I immediately struck up a friendship. He was also a pastor. His heart was for Jesus and it showed. He was a kind man. Every morning, he would stop by my classroom with a good morning wish. He knew I was newly married.

One particular morning, I must have had worry written all over my face. He asked what was bothering me. Now normally, I'm not just going to tell a random painter I can't get pregnant. But that morning, I shared with him my desire to have a child and my worry about it not happening. I believe that the Holy Spirit promptd me to reveal this personal truth to this kind man. God had something to show me.

He quickly responded with, "Can I pray with you about it?" At that point in my life, I can honestly say that I had not had many people ever ask me to pray with them. It was not a part of my daily routine. In fact, Steve and I had not prayed together about having a child. That seems crazy to me now.

These days, prayer is my first plan of action for dreams, problems, and anything and everything. Back then, not so much. But God was about to show me how important prayer is in our lives.

I hesitantly said, "Yes."

We walked into the nearest available space we could find. It happened to be a broom closet. Before praying, he asked me what I wanted to have, a boy or a girl.

Confused, I responded, "I just want a healthy baby."

In my mind, I was thinking, *God will think I am greedy if I specifically ask for gender, won't He? I thought—you can't just ask God for specifics.*

The pastor/painter gently told me God wants us to pray specifically for what we want.

He does? I thought. I immediately said, "I want a boy who loves to hunt and fish with his daddy; I want a boy who is just like his daddy!"

Next, I heard the sweetest prayer I have ever heard. The prayer from a painter in the broom closet was the kindest words I have ever heard. He prayed like he was praying to a friend. He prayed with authority like he knew it would come true. I want to cry just writing this to you. I never realized that Jesus is my friend, that He wants the best for me and you. That moment in my life would catalyze my understanding of the power of prayer.

As I traveled home that day, I thought about that prayer in the broom closet and shared it with Steve.

The next month, I was pregnant.

Nine months later, I gave birth to a beautiful baby boy. The first words out of the obstetrician's mouth were, "He looks just like his daddy!" *God is so faithful.*

As Blake grows, the pieces of that prayer fall into place, as only God can do. He loves hunting, fishing, and has a sweet soul just like his daddy.

Now and then, I run into that sweet pastor/painter. He always asks about Blake. God designed our first meeting and every other one as well. I will be forever changed and thankful for this precious man's love for Jesus. His willingness to pray with me changed the trajectory of my life. Mark Batterson's *Draw the Circle* says this about prayer,

> If you establish a prayer routine, your life
> will be anything but routine. You will go to
> places, do things, and meet people you have
> no business going to, doing, or meeting.
> You don't need to seek opportunities. All
> you have to do is seek God. And if you seek
> God, the opportunity will seek you.

I need you to think about that the next time you feel the prompting of the Holy Spirit towards someone. I certainly do not want to ever miss out on an opportunity to pray with them for God.

To the outside world, we were the perfect family. We were in church, had a beautiful baby boy, and were in love. But I was still fighting these nagging questions. I was still hurt and angry over the death of Lee. With every milestone in my life, I would feel like something was missing. Life events like our wedding day and Blake's birth or Lee's birthday would send my heart into overdrive. I missed Lee and hated the man who killed her. Although I did not talk about it much, I was still unsettled on the inside. I wondered whether this was just the way it was always going to be.

The results of this anger inside of me would be revealed in unrelated ways. Steve and I would have small arguments and they would turn into full-blown fights. The anger in my heart would burst through at a moment's notice. I am not going to gloss over this. Hurting people hurt people, and I was hurting the ones I loved most, not to mention myself.

I feel like there are many of you out there who need to hear this.

I was covering up all the pain with too much wine and this "I don't care" attitude. I was blaming Steve for my heart problems. I was yelling at him but angry with myself. Steve and Blake did not deserve this. My conscience was telling me that I was not living up to my role of mother and wife. Although Blake was still a baby, I was scared of not being the best mother to him. I was scared that Steve would leave and I would be alone . . . again. I had to figure this out before I destroyed everything I had dreamed of all those years.

How can I get over the death of Lee?
How can I not hate the man who killed her?
How do I find out why she died?
Why am I so angry?
Why did God allow Lee to die?

Why couldn't it be me?
It Should Have Been Me . . ..

God was prompting me to find the answers to all these questions. So, I did what I was good at, and opened my mouth and started asking questions. A pastor at our church was willing to listen to me. He let me ask all the questions I had bottled up inside for so many years. He figured out pretty soon that I was determined and hard-headed, therefore every question I asked received the same response: "What does the Bible say about that?" He challenged me to find the answers for myself.

Reading the Bible was not something I had ever done before, and honestly, I saw no use in it. My opinion of the Bible was that it only told stories of events that happened a long time ago and it did not pertain to anything I was asking about or doing today. But being headstrong, which God knew, I took the challenge and started reading. I would sit on my bed, read, and cry. Why was I crying? Why was this old book causing me to cry? The Bible was coming alive. It was as if the words were jumping off the pages and squeezing my heart, my soul. *How could this be; what was it about this old book that was affecting me in this way?* I could not explain it at the time, but I pressed on. I was changing. I was healing. I was being comforted by God, through His Words.

As God does so many times, the first step in my healing process was to look at myself.

My heart had to change, and the only one who could do that was Jesus.

I had to forgive myself. I had to face all those bad choices I'd made and ask God to forgive me. All those mistakes were weighing me down like a ton of bricks. I did not think God would forgive me. I thought judgment was coming to me for all those sins, and I was doomed.

If I am being perfectly honest, I was scared of God. I thought He was angry with me and if I faced Him, He would remind me of every terrible mistake I had made, every stupid decision I had made, and every sin I'd committed against Him.

As I discovered the truth in God's Word, nothing could be farther from the truth. As I forgave myself, years, and years of regret and shame that had weighed down my spirit were removed.

I think many people have no idea of the grace and mercy God is willing to give us. I certainly did not understand it at the time.

God told me through His Word that all was forgiven. By the way, Steve was telling me that too. He continually reminded me to stop looking back and move forward, but I had to see it in God's Word to believe it! I had to get right with the Lord and stop dwelling on my past. I had to accept His forgiveness, and I finally did.

The forgiveness that I received from God changed my perspective. His forgiveness allowed me the freedom to move forward and to quit looking back. Once I accepted it, I had to face the questions that had plagued me for years. I now had the tools I needed to find the answers. I knew God's Word, had the love of Steve, and the strength of my Heavenly Father.

WHY DID LEE HAVE TO DIE?

This is the question I had been asking myself for years. People would attempt to answer this with quotes they had heard along the way: "Everything happens for a reason," or "God has a plan." But here is the truth: Satan killed Lee, not God. Satan worked through that young man, his drug addiction, and his brokenness, and Satan killed my sister. There aren't any other answers to this question.

Deuteronomy 29:29
The Lord our God has secrets known to no one.
We are not accountable for them.

I think it is really important that as Christians we don't try to put words in God's mouth. When we take away from or add to God's Word, we can frustrate, mislead, and even hurt others who are searching for answers. As Jesus' followers, we need to know God's words and carefully answer these sensitive questions using God's words as they have been given to us.

Deuteronomy 4:2
You shall not add to the word which I am
commanding you, nor take away from it, that you
may keep the commandments of the Lord your
God which I command you.

Let me also explain, not for one minute do I think anyone was trying to hurt me or mislead me with those answers to my questions. I believe all of these people had love in their hearts and meant well. I am just urging us to be careful when we counsel people. I am also urging us to take God at His word. There are some things we will never fully understand on this side of heaven, I do know this: my God is loving, caring, faithful, and full of power, strength, and forgiveness. I trust Him enough to obey Him and accept His ways.

BUT WHY DID GOD ALLOW IT?

My answer to this question is firm every time I am asked.

I do not know! We serve a God who is full of grace, love, and mercy. He does not wish for any of us to experience loss or suffering, but His Word says we will have troubles. I am going to let God be God and I'll be Paige.

John 16:33
I have told you these things, so that in me you may have peace. In this world, you will have trials and sorrows. But take heart! I have overcome the world.

He doesn't say we may or we might, His Word says *we will* have trials and sorrows. I wish John had written, "In this world, everyone else but Paige will have trials and sorrows," but he did not. (*I hate it when that happens.*) Trusting in God's Word gives you peace unlike anything else this world offers. And in trusting Him, I have peace in knowing that Lee is just fine. She is with Jesus. Now, doesn't that sound good about right now?

I pray as you read this book if you do not know this peace, that you would ask Jesus to help you find it. I do not know why Lee had to die, but knowing God has a plan for my life gives me peace. I guess that is why I so desperately want to stay in His will. I ask Jesus regularly to make the Father's demands of me known. I cannot miss the plan He has for me. I do know this: as a result of Lee's death, I am writing this book and speaking to you about God, about forgiveness, and His grace. Lee would be proud, and God is pleased.

MORE QUESTIONS:
If the man that murdered my sister asked for forgiveness would he receive the same mercy and grace that I received for my sins? Would he be in heaven?

My first response in my head was always, *He most certainly will not! I am not and will not share heaven with him. Okay, God, my sins are bad, but they aren't that bad. God, I haven't killed anyone and besides, You do not want him in heaven with You anyway.*

These are the conversations I would have with my heavenly Father when this question would present itself. Then I would throw Scripture at Him. It would sound something like this. "And anyhow, Lord, the Old Testament says, 'Thou shall not kill'! So, there is no way, right Lord?"

There are times in our lives when back-and-forth conversations with God are important and helpful; a lot of times in my case. I like to think He likes it, even appreciates it. It helps us build that relationship with our Father that He so desperately wants with all of us. He knows I am strong-willed, He made me this way. However, I don't think God is going to allow me to tell Him who He can let into heaven. Frankly, I do not think it is any of my business.

Jesus' Sermon on the Mount taught me that revenge is not up to me. We are not to dwell on paybacks or revenge. Jesus is in charge of all that. Proverbs 24 says, "And don't pay them back for what they've done to me! I'll get even with them!" (Prov. 24:29). These thoughts used to haunt me and spark bitterness and anger in me, but no more. I have been freed of all that by the power of Jesus. I choose to trust Him, and that is that. When I walk through those gates of heaven, I am sure that this question will be the last thing on my mind. I have a Savior and a sister to see, and that is all that matters.

John 10:10
The thief's purpose is to steal and kill and destroy.
My purpose is to give them a rich and satisfying life.

This has become one of my favorite verses in the Bible. Satan comes to steal and kill. Satan wants us to remember our past. He wants us to feel guilty. He wants us to dwell on our mistakes and failures. Satan wanted me to feel really bad about my past so that I would single-handedly ruin my precious marriage. He wanted my anger and hate for the man who murdered my sister to continue to fester and ruin my marriage and my life. He wanted me to mess up, again and again, to keep me as far away from God and the abundant life as he could. God wants me to have a great life indeed! He is the forgiver of it all. If we place our faith in Him and ask Him to forgive us, He will do it.

Through this process of asking for and accepting forgiveness, I've changed. Now, I heard the songs growing up saying God would change us and He would break all the chains. However, I would not have fully believed it unless it happened to me.

Thank You, Jesus, for this truth! It is true—Jesus changed my heart. My forgiveness from Him gave me freedom; not the freedom to do anything I wanted but the freedom to live a life free of regret and bitterness. If we never remove the hate in our own hearts, we will never recognize the love that God is literally dying to give us all.

This transformation of my heart has been extraordinary. God knew my future depended on it and He had plans. I just did not know them yet. He has plans for you too. We must all purge ourselves of anger and focus on Christ. The work of salvation means that your life changes drastically. I no longer looked at things the same way. My desires are new and the old things, old habits lost their power.

But I still had questions, so . . . I kept searching!

5

~

Hope

"God has placed inside us all a ray of possibility."
(Jeff Bumgardner from his song "Hope"
on his Choir Project titled *God of Our Praise.*)

Y ou know how you wake up and your mind is automatically focused on something or someone? Like after the first date in high school, and you wake up thinking about every moment of that date. Well, that's what happened to me. Continuing to absorb God's Word, I would wake up early every morning with one thought, one word, one phrase, one idea in my mind.

Forgive.

Forgive who—him? At first, I ignored it. For days and weeks, I ignored it. But then my daily Bible study would take me to verses like Colossians 3:13, which says to make allowances for each other's faults and forgive *anyone* who offends you. Remember, the Lord forgave you, so you must forgive others.

I began to wonder: *Why am I constantly thinking about this?* So, I began praying about it. I've learned that when you wonder about things, it is always a good idea to pray and ask God why. He doesn't put ideas, dreams, or thoughts in our heads for no reason. So, when we are troubled our first step should be to ask Him. This was the first step of my ongoing conversation with Jesus.

"God, You really don't want me to forgive the man who killed Lee, do You? Lord, I know what Your Word says about this."

Then I would repeat it back to Him like He needed to be reminded of His Words.

"You say anyone who offends you, but You aren't really saying anyone to me, Right? God, You just mean anyone besides a man who murders a nineteen-year-old girl in the prime of her life for no reason. You do not really mean all when You say all. And besides God, You also say an eye for an eye."

I love how I threw God's words back into His face. I am sure He got a good laugh at that one.

"I know You love me, God, and You would never ask me to do that. Fathers are supposed to make everything better, so You just handle him the way I think You should handle him and that will make everything perfect. You destroy him for me. You handle it. I know what You instruct us to do, but certainly, You do not want me to forgive the man who killed my best friend, my soul mate, my sister. Lord, he isn't even sorry for what he did, and I hate him."

For months, this constant exchange with Jesus consumed my mind. Fear took over every time I got up the nerve to actually whisper the words, "I forgive him!" You see, that same insecure girl from my past still lived inside of me— that girl who always cared about what people thought— *what would people say if I told them I forgave the man who murdered Lee?* They would think that I did not love Lee, or that I had excused what he did. They would think of it as a betrayal.

God whispered, *"It's not about them or him. It is about Me."*

I thought, *how is it not about him; he does not deserve my forgiveness.* My mind would race. *How would my parents react? My daddy will be so mad at me. What would my friends say? They are going to think I've gone off the deep end about this Jesus thing. Would Steve understand?*

Insecurity and fear are the tools that Satan was using against me. He always has, he probably always will. His playbook is always the same with me. Maybe he uses them on you, too. Satan knows my insecurities. He was not going to let up on me. He did not want me to forgive anyone for anything. He was pulling out all the stops to block me from Almighty God and His abundant plan for my life. But I pressed on.

Finally, after weeks of battle, I pushed through my fears and insecurities and whispered to God that I forgave the man who murdered Lee. I said it to Jesus and to no one else, *"I forgive him."*

This was one of the first times I can recall ever knowing that a decision I was making was entirely God's will for me. It was the first decision I made solely for God without caring what anyone else thought. Fear was there, insecurity was alive, but I knew for a fact that God had told me to do this, and it was a feeling I will never forget.

Experiencing God's approval, His "atta girl," was something that I had never experienced. It is what drives me to want to do more for Him, to be a living sacrifice for Him daily. God gives us victories to build holy confidence in us. And boy did He give me confidence.

Now I know some theologian-type people will say we don't have to do anything to win God's approval, and they are absolutely correct. We do not. It is by faith alone, through Christ alone, that we are saved by grace alone. But God is my Father. He made me. He knows how I am wired. He knows I seek His approval, just like any daughter seeks her daddy's approval; just as I seek Steve's approval.

Nevertheless, I was nervous about others' reactions. I kept this decision to myself for a long time. But God had plans.

There was a homecoming service at church one day in October and the sermon was on forgiveness. That was the day I publicly went forward and gave it all to Jesus. I gave the bitterness, the anger, the resentment, the fear, and all my insecurities to Him. The pastor had a big trash can at the altar. His sermon spoke of writing the name of someone we needed to forgive and literally throwing it away. So, I wrote the murderer's name on a piece of paper and threw it in that trash can. It was freeing. I know it seems kind of silly, but it felt good.

You see, God's shoulders are the only ones strong enough to carry the load I was carrying. I was finally free of *all* of it. When God tells us to give it *all* to Him, He means *all*. He doesn't just want 95 percent of your guilt, shame, hurt, and bitterness, He wants 100 percent of it. God required my obedience so He could use it. He requires all of yours, too. I surrendered *all* to Him that Sunday morning, and I wasn't taking it back. Not this time. What I didn't realize at the time was that my surrender had the power of the Holy Spirit behind it. It was more powerful than I would ever imagine.

After church, we headed home just like every Sunday. I was so excited to share my decision of forgiveness with Steve. He was going to be the first person to know and it was going to be a great celebration. However, the conversation did not go as planned. In fact, we argued about it. Steve did not agree with my decision and did not hold his opinion back. He told me that it was ridiculous to forgive Lee's murderer and that he would never support my decision. He could not believe that I would even consider such a thing. I'd expected to get pushback from people, but I was completely caught off guard by the swiftness of Satan's attacks. And it was coming from Steve—the man I loved with all my heart, the father of my son—I was so hurt.

Now, in the past, I would have blown my top, yelled, and stomped my feet. However, I knew I was in God's will and I knew God was not going to forsake what I had done for Him. This is the beauty of knowing God's Word, of knowing the Father. That is the peace the Bible teaches us. I knew God had told me to do this, and so I also knew God would not leave me on the other side of it. He wasn't going to lead me to forgive the man who murdered my sister and then leave me alone and divorced. So, to have peace between, Steve and I agreed to disagree.

I admit it was hard to do. I have a really hard time letting things go. I'm sure you can relate. Weeks went by and I prayed. I kept my mouth closed and prayed. God was working on me, and once again I had no choice but to obey. In my waiting on Steve to come around, God was prompting me to tell the man who murdered Lee that I had forgiven him. In my quiet time, I would pull up his prison photo, and pray for guidance from God. I prayed for help. Looking at his face in the photo did not bring up the hatred it once did. I would cry as I looked at him and pray. It was hard. I began seeing him through different eyes. God was working.

So, I woke up one morning and got a piece of paper and a pen and I wrote a letter to the man who murdered Lee. All those years of stored up nasty thoughts and words I was going to tell him if I ever had the chance . . . vanished. None of those things were written. This letter was written by God and for God. It took only a few moments from my morning. I told him I forgave him. I told him what he did was wrong and that his evil deed had changed my life forever. I told him I missed my beautiful sister and I was sad. I also told him God would show him mercy and grace if he gave his life to Jesus; that he could seek forgiveness if he chose to.

I sealed it and sent it. It was finished!

Again, I did not tell anyone. I knew I couldn't tell Steve. *Would he be mad?* I was scared of his reaction; of everyone's reaction. There was that fear again. But I knew that God was with me. I was not alone in this. God was leading me and I was following.

God wants our obedience because He knows what is best for His children. Obedience can be as simple as helping someone cross the street, and as hard as forgiving someone who did not even say they were sorry. God understands our hearts better than we think we do. He knows bitterness and hatred can wiggle their way in and spread like kudzu on an old farmhouse. My heart had been consumed with hatred for so long. It was who I was for so many years, I'd become unrecognizable to myself. God changed all that. He told me to forgive and I did just that. Now, I've changed. I had hope for a future that I did not even think was possible. The world will tell you that you are stuck with your circumstances, but God says just the opposite. He says His grace is enough. He will make all things good for those who love Him. We just have to let Him.

THE FIGHT

This change in me happened rapidly. It was abrupt. No lie. For a man like Steve, who does not do well with change and thrives on routines, dealing with this change in me was hard. During the process of me forgiving and writing the letter, Satan was at work. As I grew closer to God, Steve pulled away. I noticed but I was so focused on me, I ignored it. And to be honest, I was still aggravated by his reaction when I told him that I'd forgiven Lee's murderer.

What you need to know is that Steve is a strong, quiet man. He is as sturdy as they come, but changes make him uneasy. If I tell him I want to eat dinner early, he proclaims that I put a wrench in the plans. He gets his haircut every two weeks and has watched the same three movies over and over for our entire marriage. That man loves a routine, and I love him for that.

The closer I got to God, the farther away Steve moved. It began with him sleeping downstairs on the couch. At first, he just fell asleep, no big deal, but then it was constant. Hey, it didn't bother me, I was reading my Bible. I saw that Steve and I were going in two separate directions, but I did not know what to do. I did know this: Satan was ready to steal and kill again, but this time he was in a battle with a girl who recognized his playbook and knew that God was her shield and sword.

For months, our marriage was in a mess. We were strangers in our own home. I had changed from the inside out. And, although I was at peace with myself for the first time in my life, Steve wanted the "old Paige" back. I could not understand what was going on, but I did understand who was causing it. Satan was on the attack. Ephesians 6:12 tells us that we are not fighting against flesh and blood, but against the powers of this dark world and against the spiritual forces of evil in the heavenly realms. That would be Satan folks. I was not fighting Steve, the man I love, it was Satan who was trying to destroy our marriage. Nevertheless, it would infuriate me every time Steve would say he didn't like this sudden change in me. I couldn't understand why he wouldn't want me to finally have joy and hope and peace. Everybody else seemed to take notice. Everyone else was proud of me and what I had overcome. Why not Steve?

What I now realize is that Steve was grieving the loss of the wife he once knew. He could not understand the change—the forgiveness. Remember, he is the man who hates change. We were in trouble: we were fighting and distant. It was bad. We were arguing daily, mostly under our breaths, or through text messages, to protect Blake from the shrapnel of our battles. However, I knew God did not want me to give up. I knew God was with me. I had that peace we have talked about, but I was devastated. I would scream out to God, "What in the world, Lord? I did what You asked and now my marriage is falling apart? Are You serious, Lord?" My regular conversations with God would continue.

"I obeyed *You,* and now I am going to lose the love of my life?" "Jesus, You say we will have troubles in this life, but how could this be happening?"

Steve was the answer to all my prayers, the man of my dreams. We had a perfect little family and now we had God right in the center of it. Everything should have been perfect. This conflict between us was the playbook of Satan, the thief. Thieves always attack when you least expect it.

This was exactly the right time for an attack from Satan. We were both confused, mad, and hurt. I doubted everything I had done, and Steve seemed to be finished. This was the perfect timing for the accuser to come in and strike. But remember that girl who begged for love, who apologized when she wasn't even wrong? She was gone. Jesus had changed her and had changed her for such a time as this! Working my way through all those questions, studying God's Word prepared me for just this moment. God knew this was coming and He had already equipped me to deal with it the right way. I knew I had to stand firm. I *knew* I had to be still and let God do His thing. If you are in a tight spot in a relationship right now, you may need to hear this. I am a control freak. Are you? It is ok to admit it. I have a million things going on at a time. I am a wife, mom, daughter, principal, a leader at my church, a teacher of the Word, a public speaker, and now an author. Just writing that made me exhausted. I wanted to fix Steve and fix our marriage right then. I did not want to wait. I did not want to listen. But God was in control, not me, not us. I am so thankful that this time, I listened to Him. I let God do His thing. It was hard. My controlling self did not want to wait, but this time I did, and let me tell you it was worth the wait. Keep reading, it turns out better than I ever expected.

One night during one of our more heated arguments, Steve confided in me that God told him to leave me and Blake. Thank God, I had His words written on my heart at this very moment. The benefit of knowing the Bible is that when you are faced with statements like this, you can go to battle with your shield and armor, without worrying about being defeated. I challenged Steve and asked him to consider that it was Satan talking to him, not God. Jesus would never tell him to leave Blake and me, I challenged Steve, saying "God's character would never tell you to leave me."

Steve left. We arranged it so Blake would not suspect anything. They both went hunting one weekend. Steve told Blake he was staying a few extra nights and that Blake should come home. I met them at an exit on I-20. It was a rainy November day and as I parked off the road to wait on them, I wondered if Steve would stick to the plan. I hoped and prayed he would hug me and tell me he was coming home. I watched them as they drove up in Steve's old red truck. My heart was breaking. I was devastated. Blake jumped in my car, not suspecting anything. Steve stayed in his truck and pulled up to my window. He looked at me with those beautiful green eyes filled with tears. Without saying a word, he drove off. I watched his old truck go down that dirt road, my heart was broken. As I write this, the lump in my throat remains.

I remember driving home that day, crying silently, and praying to God for help. "Highway 20 Ride" by the Zac Brown Band was playing in my head. Listen to it if you have never heard it, but have a tissue handy. Blake was hungry, so we stopped at Steak 'n Shake on the way home. It's our favorite burger place. I tried to choke back my feelings and act as if nothing was wrong.

Blake knew something was up and asked, "What's wrong, Mommy?" I can still hear him saying it.

Blake and I are very close. He has taken the role of my protector. I don't know if it is normal or not for a son to feel this way, but mine does, and that is fine with me. He can read my face better than anyone. Blake is very intuitive and is never afraid to ask me questions. I lied and told him I was fine. I probably said that I was just tired.

Why was this happening? I did not want Blake to grow up without his daddy. I wanted Steve beside me until we were old and grey. We had dreams. We'd made plans for the future.

Several times, I picked up the phone to call Steve. I knew what I would say. "Just forget it! I'll stop with all this forgiveness and Bible reading if you will just come home!" I will go back to the "old Paige" and it will be fine.

But that would have been a lie. I could not say those words out loud. I could not disobey God. So, I prayed and prayed. I was not giving up on us and I certainly was not giving up on God. I knew without a shadow of a doubt that God was not going to leave us. I knew if I stood firm in my faith, God would protect us. The loving God I knew would not have told me to forgive and just leave me hanging. He was not finished with me yet!

This wasn't about Steve's faith; it was about my faith.

First Peter chapter 3 says, "Wives must accept the authority of your husbands so that if any of them do not believe the Word, they may be won over without words but by the behavior of their wives" (1 Peter 3:1–2). Now, I am not saying that Steve was not a Christian. He'd placed his faith in Jesus years prior. In fact, we were baptized together, and that was one of the most precious moments in our lives together. After we'd discovered that I was pregnant with Blake, Steve confided in me that he'd never been baptized as a child. I was raised Methodist and was never baptized by submersion. We decided to rededicate our lives to Christ together and were baptized with Blake in my belly. It was such a special moment in our lives.

There are times when couples walk with God at different paces. I think this happens more often than not. I knew my faith had to be the solution, that my faith was the answer. So, I had to be strong and fight for my marriage. I knew I had the Holy Spirit in my corner. Now, don't think for a minute that my faith was so strong that I knew with 100 percent confidence everything was going to turn out okay. I did not. But it only takes a mustard seed, right?

After a few days, Steve came home from the woods, but we were definitely not out of the woods yet as a family. Steve was in turmoil. He began having panic attacks, and we were falling apart. I cried myself to sleep a lot of nights, hiding the reality from family and friends. In fact, a lot of my family and friends will be learning about our struggle as they read this book, just as you are.

Another important lesson I have learned through God's Word is self-control. Now the "old Paige" would have called every person she knew to gossip about her marriage and get everyone on her side. Through my faith, I have learned that at times it is best to only talk to God. I have discovered the world will give you advice that does not line up with God's Word. The few friends I did confide in were turning me straight back to Scripture and became my prayer warriors. This only confirms the importance of surrounding yourself with Jesus-loving men and women.

Doubt and fear consumed me. How could I have gone from the mountaintop to the valley at the same time? I loved Jesus and believed people were supposed to be happy and everything was going to be rainbows and roses from here on out. Well, tell that to Jesus. He was baptized and immediately tempted in the wilderness. I could relate. I had experienced God's powerful mercy and grace and then my husband headed for the woods. Literally!

Steve and I struggled for a year after I forgave the man who murdered Lee. We tried our best to keep our problems from Blake, the family, and our friends. But God saw, He listened, and He healed. Satan threw temptations and lies at us from every direction. I experienced such lows that it became unbearable at times, but God stood guard. God protected us in ways that only He could. I saw it. I knew it.

As God was creating and forming the earth, the Bible says He hovered over the waters. I felt God hovering over us. His spirit hovers over you, too. Steve's heart slowly began to soften and so did mine. News flash: Steve wasn't the only guilty party in the fight. I made mistakes too. I love how God uses *all* things for His glory. He changes us in our tribulations for the . . .

better
every
single
time!

I wonder how many times this happens to couples. How many times does one spouse run smack into a Holy Spirit thunderclap, and the other spouse just feels a little sprinkle of the Spirit? I expected Steve to accept the new me, to understand my forgiveness, and be proud of me immediately.

Although that did not happen the way I planned, it did happen the way God planned it. As I reflect on my actions during our struggle, I was abrasive, and in Steve's face a lot. I was demanding that he understand, and that is not the way to show God's love to anyone, especially to your husband. Coming to a common understanding did not happen overnight either. It took time for us to heal and to forgive. But it did happen.

God is so very good.

Steve and I are happier and stronger in our marriage than we have ever been. Steve is proud of me! He not only tells me, but his spirit shows it, and that is all God's work. Being on the other side of this, I see God's hands all over it. I see Steve praying openly with Blake and me. I see changes in him that I never thought possible. I don't even mention it to him when I notice something, I just whisper, "Thank You" to God, and enjoy the moment. I see Steve loving me in ways I never imagined! As I am writing this book, he leans in to kiss my cheek and whispers, "I am proud of you!" My faith in God has paid off in dividends that are more precious to me than gold. Steve has become a Godly example to Blake and me. I learn from him daily. I love Steve more today than I did on our wedding day. It is true: the more you love God, the more you love, the more you are loved.

Matthew 6:14–15
*For if you forgive other people when they sin
against you, your heavenly Father will also forgive you.
But if you do not forgive others their sins,
your Father will not forgive your sins.*

My obedience took faith. We teach about faith and we talk about faith, but when you put feet to your faith, lives change. God was shouting at me through my heartache to forgive. I could have ignored His shouting and lived a decent life with heartache and regret. But I chose to obey God and forgive. I choose to believe in God and all of His promises. His Word says He is faithful, and He will never let me go. When I am weak, I call on these promises. That is why knowing God's Word is so important. He doesn't need me calling out Scripture to Him, but it sure helps me understand His expectations and express my own concerns. His Word can help you too.

Psalm 73:23–24
Yet I am always with you; you hold me by my right hand. You guide me with your counsel, and afterward, you will take me into glory.

Forgiveness is not about reasoning with God. It is only about your obedience to your Father. God doesn't give suggestions in the Bible, He commands. Once you take that first step to forgive, He will do the rest. Just like when God commanded in the third chapter of Joshua "When you reach the banks of the Jordan River, you take the first steps into the river and stop there" (Josh. 3:80). After the Israelites' obedience, the flow of the river stopped and dried up, so they could cross. We have to take that first step of faith. We have to put away our pride, our hatred, our feelings, and just take the first step. Our obedience has the power of the Holy Spirit behind it. It is unstoppable, and the things God will do with our obedience to Him are unimaginable.

Are you ready? Take that first step into the Jordan river and see what is on the other side.

THE NOBLEST REVENGE IS TO FORGIVE.

My life today is unlike anything I could have imagined for myself. I thought I was doomed to grieve and muddle through, doing the best I could with what life had dealt me. I know someone reading this book thinks the same thing about their own life. I am here to tell you, *It ain't true*. No matter what has happened to you, no matter who has hurt you, no matter what you have done, God is bigger. He is bigger than your divorce. He is bigger than your addiction or your mistakes. He is bigger and more powerful than bitterness, rage, or sin. He is also bigger than that hole in your heart that was created by the loss of a loved one, a soul mate, a child, a sister. God will fill up that space with an unending amount of love and compassion. You just have to let Him.

God promises that if we delight in Him, He will give us the desires of our hearts. I know this is true, I've seen it play out so many times, especially in recent years.

I kept asking God for a close circle of friends. It wasn't that I didn't have any friends; I have many friends I've known practically all my life, and I love them with all my heart. But, as I grew in my faith, I needed someone to walk along with me. I needed new friends who would point me to Scripture and counsel me when I needed it. The struggles of being a strong Christian woman are real, and I needed others to walk alongside me. By the way, you need this too. I started praying for godly women to come into my life: women who would understand my struggles and wanted to study God's Word as much as I did; women I could be completely honest with about my struggles and who would not be judgmental.

Well, cue the "better than you could imagine" blessing from Jesus. As I undertook my walk of faith, God put me in the path of the most amazing women. A woman I admired from a distance in my church messaged me out of the blue sky one day and asked to meet. She asked me to be a part of a discipleship group with her and three other women. I immediately said, "Yes!" This was the beginning of a friendship that has blossomed and grown into one of my most valuable possessions: not only with her but with the other women too.

I am now surrounded by women I can trust and lean on. These women have spoken prophecy in my life. These five women have all played a big part in why I am writing this book today. I can look back and see God's hand in meeting each of them. I am aware of how they all collectively and individually add to my life abundantly. We pray for and encourage each other. Our chain of texts messages are a gift from God Himself. God will always honor these friendships.

Your desires and prayers should be to fulfill the will of God in your life and then trust that He will tell you, or better yet, show you His plan. 'Cause He will. He led me to that church business meeting I spoke about at the beginning of my story, He undeniably made me speak up, and He formed the words that came out of my mouth that day. Those words spoken by my now-pastor, Stephen, would be the beginning of my new prayers. I never expected to speak at the church meeting. I never expected to blurt out my testimony, but God expected it. In fact, He designed it.

He is the great I AM.

And on that day, He said, I AM going to change the trajectory of Paige's life, and she will know and live out Romans 8:28 forever: "And we know that God causes EVERYTHING to work together for the GOOD of those who love God and are called according to His purpose for them" (emphasis mine).

I am currently reading a devotional by Mark Batterson, *Draw the Circle*. (Zondervan 2012). In his devotional, he says: "You may not see yourself as a prophet, but you are one. You're a prophet to your friends." He elaborates and says "your words have the potential to change lives by helping people discover their identity and destiny in Jesus Christ." I believe Pastor Stephen did just that in that church business meeting. The prayers and words by my God-given friends combined with the insight of my pastor and, when encompassed by God's sovereignty, changed the course of my life.

A few months later, Pastor Stephen and I made a testimonial video. This video has been viewed somewhere between 70,000 and 80,000 times on social media. God has allowed me to start a ministry about forgiveness and grace. He has allowed me to begin a speaking ministry. I now have the awesome opportunity to speak at area churches and women's events about the power of forgiveness. God has given me opportunities and dreams I would have never imagined in my former life. He has given me prayers I would have never prayed. I pray big prayers, for big, impossible dreams. Writing this book has been a God-given dream that only He could have helped me accomplish. Just as I knew God had told me to forgive, I also know He told me to write this book. I don't know how this book will sell or serve my readers, but He knows, and that is all that matters.

Establishing a ministry and speaking at churches and women's events has been a God-given dream that only He could help me accomplish. As I speak to groups, I still laugh and think: *What in the world am I doing up here?* Having a ministry that will change the way others think about forgiveness and God's grace is a dream that only He can fulfill. In the past, I would pray for God to change the people around me, to take the pain away, to make others pay for what they had done to me. I wanted the man who murdered my sister to die. My heart was full of anger and hatred, and I wanted God to make him hurt too. But God said, "No, ma'am. Let's do it *my* way." My obedience to God changed my prayer life, my dreams, my future. Obedience to His Word and extravagant forgiveness can change your life too.

Helping others know Him and His love is my new passion. Think about it: it could be your new passion too! Colossians 3 says, "You used to do these things [sexual immorality, drunkenness, impurity, lust, evil desires, greed, idolatry] when your life was still part of this world. But now is the time to get rid of anger, rage, malicious behavior, slander, and dirty language [and may I add for my benefit, hate]" (Col. 3:7–8 author's paraphrase). If you pray to God to help you accomplish this, He will give you a new nature, a renewed heart, a new life. God's grace will train us, teach us, and redeem us. We just have to ask.

No one wants to hear a sermon; they want to *see* a sermon. Be that sermon for someone.

My life is not perfect. Steve and I still have struggles, just like every other couple. But what I understand now is that all I have to do is plant seeds of love and grace in my home, and God will do the harvesting. Billy Graham said, "It is the Holy Spirit's job to convict. God's job to judge, and my job to love." (Billy Graham Quotes, www.goodreads.com) Being all judgmental to others is not the answer. *Love is!* And while we are on the subject of Billy Graham, he also says that you can't pray for someone and hate them at the same time. (Billy Graham Quotes, www.goodreads.com) That is the truth. If you hate someone, do God a favor and begin praying for them. This act of obedience will change your perspective. And that is what God is after. And if you don't believe Billy Graham, believe Jesus. Matthew chapter 5 says,

> So if you are presenting a sacrifice at the altar in the Temple and you suddenly remember that someone has something against you [or you have something against them], leave your sacrifice there at the altar. Go and be reconciled to that person. Then come and offer your sacrifice to God." (Matthew 5:23–24 author's paraphrase)

In other words, if you have hate in your heart, then your prayers are bouncing off the walls in heaven.

This is what I know:

The man who murdered my sister should remain in prison. He must pay his debt to society.

My forgiveness was not easy; it was hard. If you have someone to forgive, it will be hard for you, too. I don't want anyone to assume that any of this was easy. There are days when I have to forgive him over and over again. I hear a song or watch a movie and I am reminded of Lee. I look in the mirror and wonder how she would look, what would she have named her children. I miss Lee! I get sad. I long for her.

Evil changed my family's life. It changed my life. That single evil act has affected generations. During quiet times, I think about it. I think about Lee. This past May 4 would have been Lee's fifty-first birthday, and I cried all day. And guess what? That is okay. I can allow myself to feel that pain, I just can't stay there. I've lost a lifetime of love and happiness to share with Lee but

I've got a life worth living, and God has big plans for me.

I lost a lot.

But my attitude and perspective are everything.

Bitterness is just one bad attitude away.

Jesus has to be everything. He has to be everything to you too.

Forgiveness does not mean that I excuse what Lee's murderer did. I do not!

But God has given me a story to share with you. Speaking about Lee gives me pure joy! And that is a God-given thing!

Romans 8:28 says that God uses all things. All things like murder, death, divorce, strife, abuse, war, fighting.

All things can be used for His glory if we just obey!

Don't give that "thing" in your life the power to control you, as I did for so many years.

Think about it like this: if that "thing" was right in front of you now, would you honor it? Would you put it on your mantle and frame it? No, you would not. So, stop dwelling on it, stop worshiping your pain, heartache, hatred, and bitterness. Allow Jesus to take it, just like I did. Allow Him to carry it, not just for a minute or two, but forever!

Give the power, the worship to Jesus!

Will you give your bitterness, anger, hurt, resentment to God today?

Forgiveness is a choice—it is something you can do today!

Please don't say, "I am working on it," or "It is not the right time!" And for Pete's sake, do not say, "Paige is way stronger than I am. I could not do what she did." That is simply not true! That is a lie, because, on my own, I am a weak, insecure woman; but with Him, I am fearless and strong.

I want to leave you with one last verse to dwell on. It is from the book of Daniel and it is my new favorite verse (as you may have picked up on, I have many new favorite verses).

Daniel 10:12
Don't be afraid, Daniel. Since the first day you began to pray for understanding and to humble yourself before your God, your request has been heard in heaven.

Now, if that doesn't get your blood pumping, I don't know what will. I went from being a scared little girl saying, I am a nobody to believing 2 Samuel 7:18 was written just for me. "Then King David went in and sat before the Lord and prayed, 'Who am I, O Sovereign Lord, and what is my family, that You Have Brought Me Thus Far?" He will bring you "thus far" as well.

Thank you for taking the time to read my little book. I am praying for you. I pray that you will obey God and forgive that person or persons who have offended or hurt you. I pray my words will give you the strength and hope to face the giants in your life. I pray you will use this book to help others, as I have tried to do. I pray that you ask God for big dreams and that you will trust God to answer them. I pray we will all make it our life's mission to glorify God by our actions, reactions, and our testimonies. My story can be your story too, with God's extraordinary GRACE anything is possible.

CPSIA information can be obtained
at www.ICGtesting.com
Printed in the USA
BVHW090808030321
601532BV00003B/10